Symbols of Freedom

National Parks

Great Smoky Mountains National Park

Peggy Pancella

Heinemann Library
Chicago, Illinois

Customer Service 888-454-2279
Visit our website at www.heinemannlibrary.com

Page layout by Ron Kamen and edesign
Photo research by Maria Joannou and Erica Newbery
Illustrations by Martin Sanders
Printed and bound in China by South China Printing Company Limited

10 09 08 07 06
10 9 8 7 6 5 4 3 2 1

Library of Congress Cataloging-in-Publication Data
Pancella, Peggy.
  Great Smoky Mountains National Park / Peggy Pancella.
    p. cm. -- (Symbols of freedom)
  Includes bibliographical references and index.
  ISBN 1-4034-7796-5 (library binding - hardcover)
  1. Great Smoky Mountains (N.C. and Tenn.)--Juvenile literature. 2. Great Smoky Mountains National Park (N.C. and Tenn.)--Juvenile literature. I. Title. II. Series.
  F443.G7P36 2006
  917.68'89--dc22
                                        2005026573

Acknowledgments
The author and publishers are grateful to the following for permission to reproduce copyright material:
Alamy Images pp. 11 (Danita Delimont), 20 (Photo Network), 24 (Danita Delimont); Corbis pp. 5 (Raymond Gehman), 8 (Raymond Gehman), 9 (W. Cody), 13 (David Muench), 14, 16 (David Muench), 21 (David Muench), 22 (Raymond Gehman), 23 (Buddy Mays), 25, 26 (William A Bake), 27; Getty Images pp. 4, 10 (Stone), 15 (America 24-7); Richard Weisser and SmokyPhotos.com pp. 7, 17, 18, 19; United States Geological Survey p. 12.

Cover photograph of Great Smoky Mountains National Park reproduced with permission of Getty Images.

Every effort has been made to contact copyright holders of any material reproduced in this book.
Any omissions will be rectified in subsequent printings if notice is given to the publisher.

Some words are shown in bold, **like this**. You can find out what they mean by looking in the glossary.

Contents

Our National Parks

National parks are areas set aside for people to visit and enjoy **nature**. The land in national parks is protected. People cannot cut down trees or pick plants in a national park.

National parks belong to all the people.

There are **388** national park areas in the United States. Great Smoky Mountains National Park has the most visitors. Over nine million people visit the park each year.

Great Smoky Mountains National Park

Great Smoky Mountains National Park is in the eastern part of the United States. Half of the park is in Tennessee. The other half is in North Carolina.

The Smoky Mountains are usually covered with a blue **mist** that looks like smoke. This is where Great Smoky Mountains National Park gets its name.

The mist is mostly **water vapor** mixed with oils from the park's trees.

Great Smoky Mountains Long Ago

For thousands of years, Native Americans called the Cherokee lived in the Smoky Mountains. Then other **settlers** came. They cut down trees and grew **crops**.

This woman is doing a traditional Cherokee craft.

The John Oliver cabin in Cades Cove was built in 1820.

Some people wanted to protect the mountain plants and animals. They helped raise money to buy the land. In 1934, Great Smoky Mountains became a **national park**.

Visiting Great Smoky Mountains National Park

Great Smoky Mountains National Park is open all year. Most people visit in spring, summer, or fall. They camp, fish, hike, ride horses, and look at **wildlife**.

Some visitors go sledding.

Winters can be cold in the Smoky Mountains. Some park roads are closed because of snow. People can still go hiking and cross-country skiing.

The Smoky Mountains

The Smoky Mountains are millions of years old. At first, their tops were pointed. Over time, wind and water wore down the rock. Now their tops are rounded.

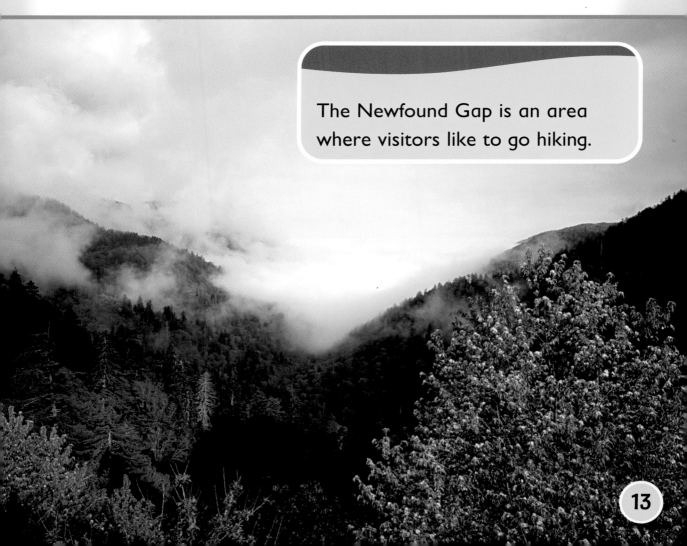

The Smokies are part of a long group of mountains called the Appalachians. This mountain **range** covers much of the eastern United States.

The Newfound Gap is an area where visitors like to go hiking.

Balds and Coves

Most of the Smoky Mountains are covered with trees. Some areas do not have any trees and are called **balds**. Some balds are **grassy**. Others with small bushes are called **heaths**.

Grassy balds are covered with grass or small flowers.

There are also low places between the mountains. These areas are called **coves**. Many **settlers** used to grow **crops** and raise animals on the flat land in the coves.

Cades Cove

Waterfalls and Streams

Laurel Falls

Great Smoky Mountains National Park has many waterfalls. Some are big and some are small. Many park visitors hike along trails to reach the beautiful waterfalls.

Fast-moving streams also flow down the rocky mountainsides. These streams are home to many kinds of animals, including fish and **salamanders**.

Forests

Great Smoky Mountains National Park is famous for its forests. More than 120 kinds of trees grow there. **Evergreen** trees such as spruce and pine cover the highest slopes.

Many people visit the park in fall to admire the colorful leaves.

Farther down, trees such as maples and oaks grow. These trees lose their leaves each fall. More than 200 kinds of birds live in the park's trees.

Other Plants

Each spring, wildflowers of every color fill the park. These beautiful flowers are very popular sights. Some park visitors count how many different kinds they find.

About 1,500 kinds of wildflowers bloom in the park.

Larger plants such as rhododendron flower on **heath balds** in spring. Sometimes these areas are called rhododendron balds. Laurel and blueberry bushes also grow there.

Rhododendron flowers are very colorful.

Animals in the Great Smoky Mountains

The park is home to many kinds of animals. Visitors often see black bears, deer, rabbits, and squirrels. Foxes, raccoons, and other animals also live here.

The black bear is one of the park's largest animals.

Sunrise and sunset are good times to see animals. Many animals come out to find food and drink. Other animals come out only at night. They are harder to spot.

You have to stay very still and quiet to see a wild turkey.

Looking into the Past

Some of the early **settlers'** buildings still stand in Great Smoky Mountains National Park. Visitors can see houses, barns, schools, churches, and other buildings.

This farm is near Oconaluftee Visitor Center.

Inside some of the buildings, workers show how the settlers used to live. They cook, weave cloth, and grind grain. They use tools and wear clothes from long ago.

Great Smoky Mountains National Park has three visitor centers with information about the park. There are also campgrounds and a lodge where visitors can stay.

Visitors come to John Davis House to see how early settlers used to live.

Park rangers work in all areas of the park. They teach people about the park's animals and plants. Sometimes they lead hikes or show visitors the park's special sights.

Map of Great Smoky Mountains National Park

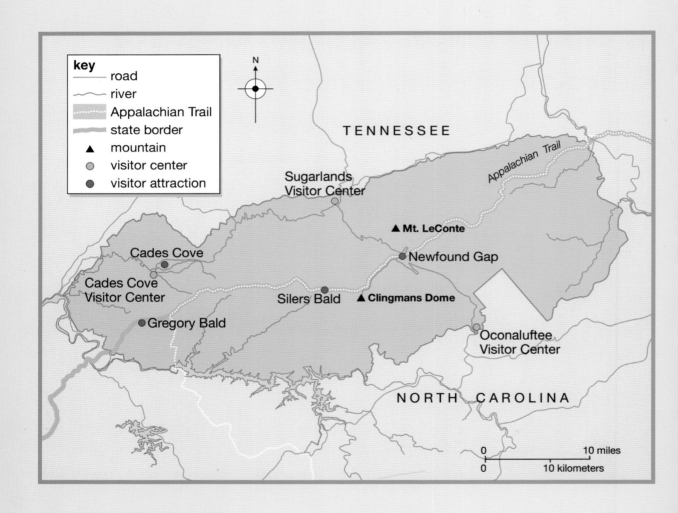

key
- —— road
- ∿∿ river
- ⋯⋯ Appalachian Trail
- ≈≈ state border
- ▲ mountain
- ● visitor center
- ● visitor attraction

N

TENNESSEE

Appalachian Trail

Sugarlands
Visitor Center

▲ Mt. LeConte

Cades Cove

● Newfound Gap

Cades Cove
Visitor Center

Silers Bald   ▲ Clingmans Dome

● Gregory Bald

Oconaluftee
Visitor Center

NORTH CAROLINA

0   10 miles
0   10 kilometers

Timeline

300 million years ago	Smoky Mountains are formed.
About 1000	Cherokee people move into the Smoky Mountains.
1540	Spanish explorer Hernando de Soto travels through the Smoky Mountains.
Late 1700s	**Settlers** begin to move into the Smoky Mountains.
1838	Settlers force most of the Cherokee to leave the area.
Early 1900s	People cut down millions of trees in the Smoky Mountains and sell the wood for money.
1926	United States **government** agrees that the area can be made into a park; people start raising money to buy the land.
1934	Great Smoky Mountains becomes a **national park**.
1940	President Franklin D. Roosevelt officially opens the park.
1976	The park is made an International Biosphere Reserve.

Glossary

bald area of a mountain where there are no trees

cove wide, flat-bottomed valley in the Smoky Mountains

crop plant grown for food or other use

evergreen tree that does not lose its leaves in the winter. Most evergreens have needlelike leaves.

government group of people that makes laws for and runs a country

grassy bald open area where grass and small plants grow instead of trees

heath bald open area on a mountain where plants grow instead of trees

mist foggy cloud in the air, usually near the ground

national park natural area set aside by the government for people to visit

nature the outdoors and the wild plants and animals found there

park ranger person who works in a national park

range group or chain of mountains

salamander small lizardlike animal that lives in or near water

settler person who moves to a new place to live

water vapor water that has changed into a gas. Vapor is cooler than steam.

wildlife wild animals of an area

Find Out More

Books

An older reader can help you with these books:

Domeniconi, David. *M Is for Majestic: A National Parks Alphabet.* Farmington Hills, Mich: Thomson Gale, 2003.

Petersen, David. *National Parks.* Danbury, Conn.: Children's Press, 2000.

Raatma, Lucia. *Our National Parks.* Mankato, Minn.: Compass Point Books, 2002.

Address

To find out more about Great Smoky Mountains National Park, write to:

Great Smoky Mountains National Park
107 Park Headquarters Road
Gatlinburg, TN 37738
Visitor Information Recorded Message:
(865) 436-1200

Website

You can visit the park's official website at:
http://www.nps.gov/grsm

Index